THE

CURSE

OF THE

STRONG

How to Overcome Narcissistic Parenting, Perfectionism, and Codependency To Avoid Burn-Out!

Deirdre Haynes, ED.S, LPCS

DEDICATION

This book is dedicated to all the "strong" people out there that constantly save the day for everyone else only to deal with their issues alone.

Dear Reader,

I see you. You are that successful educator, businesswoman, mother, or entrepreneur. You get up early, handle your business effortlessly, and take care of so many people throughout your day. **<u>Everyone can count on you</u>**. No matter what, you're the one they call when the going gets tough or problems need to be solved. You can handle it! You are focused, organized and on-point. Employers love your work ethic and commitment. Family members know that if something needs to be resolved then they can call in the big guns- YOU! Your husband/partner leans on you to emotionally support him and his issues. Your children come to you to help them make every decision. You give and give and give until now....you are exhausted! You feel as if you are at the end of your rope and you don't even have the strength anymore to tie a knot and hold on. You are tired. You are empty. You secretly feel angry and resentful because you are always there for everyone else but no one notices your pain and struggles. You feel as if you are dying inside from the drain of physical and mental exhaustion. After years and years of being there for everyone else, you are realizing that you have nothing else to give.

You, my dear, have finally hit a wall.

Now, you are in the perfect position to stop, make changes, and heal.

Let's begin.

Chapters

An Introduction

Chapter 1:   So, What Is The Curse Of The Strong?

Chapter 2:   Narcissistic Parent

2.1   Emotionally Distant

2.2   Selfish and Self-Centered

2.3   Jealous and Possessive

2.4   Master Manipulators

Vignette 1 & 2:   The Narcissistic Mother

Chapter 3:   Perfectionism

3.1   Excessive Concern Over Mistakes

3.2   Excessively High Personal Standards

3.3   High Parental Expectations

3.4   High Parental Criticism

3.5   Exaggerated Emphasis on Precision

3.6   Order and Organization

3.7   Doubts About Actions

3.8   The Dark Side Of Perfectionism

Chapters

Vignette 3 & 4:   **Perfectionism**

Chapter 4:   **Codependency**

4.1   They Take and You Give

4.2   No Benefit To You

4.3   Resentment and Guilt

Vignette 4 & 5:   **Codependency**

Chapter 5:   **The Blindspot Blueprint**

Additional Resources

Conclusion

An Introduction

Women have always been known to be self-reliant and resilient during some of the most trying times. With today's fast past world, times do not have to necessarily be trying or tough in order to cause major psychological issues within women. The prevalence of single moms, married moms that carry the brunt of running their household, or even single women with power jobs has increased. With it, the number of women experiencing anxiety, depression, and unresolved anger issues has also increased.

Thankfully, more and more of these women are scheduling mental health counseling appointments because they are at their breaking point and have realized that they do not know how to relieve or resolve their overwhelming symptoms and situations.

During my therapy sessions, the client and I search their memories to find the root of their issues. As we explore possible causes of their disorders, I have noticed a common thread among these burned-out women.

Each woman has their own individual story but the common themes that tend to lace themselves through almost all of their stories in various ways are Narcissistic Parent(s), Perfectionism, and Codependency. The characters may change in each story but there is usually one or more of these themes present.

I decided to write this book because many women are unaware of what Narcissistic Parenting, Perfectionism, and/or Codependency actually mean. They may have heard those words in passing but until they are in counseling, they have no clue of what these three components look like in the real world.

I also wrote this book to break down these complex themes and behaviors in a way that will provide the reader with a blueprint for recognizing these traits in themselves and others. This book also includes vignettes or short, descriptive examples or stories of what these themes look like in the real world. These stories are fictional and are meant to provide context. The final chapter of this book, The Blindspot Blueprint, offers various resources, tips and tools that will be highly useful in helping you take back control of your life and possibly help you avoid becoming burned-out.

As with all of my books, products, courses and services, I hope that this information is helpful to you. Let's begin.

Chapter 1:

So, What Is The Curse

Of The Strong?

So, what is the "curse of the strong"? I came up with what is now the title of this book while I was conducting a therapy session. I was talking with a young woman and it suddenly hit my brain that what she was describing were the attributes of a strong, superhuman person that was both blessed and cursed to always be the strong, stable, reliable one in her family and relationships.

I told this woman that what she was describing was indeed a **blessing and a curse**. Strong women tend to be successful women. <u>The blessing in being the "strong one" is that you are able to handle things and get things done</u>. You can be relied upon and it feels good to be able to help family, friends, and loved ones with your money, time, expertise, knowledge, and/or help.

You are able to juggle your own problems and issues while simultaneously helping others solve their own problems. You take everything in stride, keep pushing, and showing up day after day until you finally hit your own wall. This is where the curse enters the picture.

<u>The cursed part of being the "strong one" is that you are never allowed to be weak, scared, sad or tired</u>. You have never been given permission or you have never given yourself permission to make a mistake. You are rarely asked about how you are feeling about the death, or the breakup, or the stress that you are under. People automatically assume that you are ok or that you can handle it. You have probably heard those exact words being uttered to you if you have, on the rare occasion, told someone that you don't feel...okay.

There is a reason why they cannot handle or accept that you may be tired, depressed, anxious or anything other than fully charged and on standby but we will discuss that in the Codependency chapter.

The main concept that I want to drive home here is that if you have the **Curse Of The Strong** then you are sick and tired of being sick and tired with no one noticing. You are tired of selfish, self-centered people taking from you and giving little to nothing back. You are tired of being so independent that you literally can not form the words to ask for help. You have come to the realization that you put on your superwoman cape daily and help everyone else solve their problems but when you are faced with your own problems, you are all alone.

If any of this describes your current state, then let's move to the next chapter.

Chapter 2:

The Narcissistic Mother

If you have read any of my books or encountered me in the counseling arena, you know that I like to start at the beginning. **The root or core of most psychological disorders, in my opinion, start in childhood**. Your parents are essentially your first teachers. They teach us how to love, how to be loved, and show us glimpses of who we are through their eyes.

When the dynamic is askew within the parent-child relationship, then problems surface. They may not be blatant and they may not occur until later in life but trust me when I say that problems will rear their ugly heads to be dealt with at some point.

Even though the parenting dynamic can vary, meaning grandparents, aunts, and other family members can rear a child, for the purposes of this book, I am going to focus on the Mother-Daughter dynamic.

Again, this does not mean that the father, grandmother/grandfather, or aunt/uncle may not have exhibited Narcissistic tendencies. However, for ease of explanation, I chose to focus on one dynamic. You can insert whatever parent parented you if you see these same traits in that person.

Pay attention to the traits and examples presented in the following sections. The title indicates the specific trait. A vignette will follow this section to pull all these concepts together.

2.1 Emotionally Distant

The Narcissistic mother is usually not emotionally connected with her child. Emotional distance divides them due to her lack of empathy. They may or may not provide adequate material support (i.e. shelter, clothes, etc.) either since some Narcissistic mothers also neglect their child's physical needs.

If you have a Narcissistic mother, as a child you may not have been hugged or nurtured by your mother. She may have treated you as if you were something to do-like you were an object that she had to feed, clothe, take to school, etc. It is quite probable that she did not support you by attending school-wide events unless they were important enough that she would look bad if she did not go.

No one wants to believe that someone brought you into this world only to not love you or not want you.

Unfortunately, this happens daily.

Some Narcissistic mothers never tell their children that they love them. Some of you may have experienced this heartbreaking lack of verbal affirmation. Others of you may have a mother that tells you that she loves you all the time but something "feels" off.

Narcissistic mothers may say they love you and take minimal action to show you that they love you but in reality the **INTENTION** is off. They say the words and do the actions because then it proves to the world that they are a good parent.

To a Narcissistic mother, doing "right" by their child only serves to make them look good. It is like, "Hey, look at how great a person and parent I am!" So, the question begs to be asked, "Is it really about the child or is it about you?"

Most likely, when you were dealing with problems throughout your life, you may have felt that you could not talk to your mother. Most likely it was because she would make you feel like you were wrong or not good enough.

Put downs, name-calling, talking over you, interrupting you and even cursing you out may have occurred when you attempted to share your feelings especially if these feelings were not in alignment with hers. These actions taught you at an early age that you could not trust her with the tender, fragile and emotional parts of yourself.

In those lonely moments, you learned to soothe your own fears, to cry your tears in isolation, and to seek nurturing and love through other sources such as family members, teachers, partners and possibly your own children.

The reason that most Narcissistic mothers are emotionally distant from their children is that they lack empathy. **Empathy is the ability to put yourself in someone else's shoes and to feel how they feel in a particular situation.** It is not the same as sympathy in which you feel sorry for someone.

Instead, it is the act of literally taking on the emotions of someone else to the point that you feel their pain. Maybe not in the same intensity that they do but you understand intellectually and emotionally how that person feels often without them even telling you.

The empathy switch is missing in Narcissists. They will not hold you, console you, and tell you everything will be alright. Instead, they would most likely tell you to suck it up, get over it and move on no matter how devastating the event was that caused your pain.

Some will justify these actions as a pep talk but truth be told they behave in that way because the attention is not on them. They won't give you space to feel or express your pain (or issues) because they feel they should always be the center of attention.

A great way to figure out if your mother or anyone else is a Narcissist is to pay attention to how they behave when they are stressed or dealing with their own issues. If they expect you to drop everything and listen to them belabor their own issues and pain but have no interest in listening to your own pain or issues, then you are most likely dealing with a Narcissist.

2.2 Selfish and Self-Centered

This leads me to my next point. Narcissistic mothers are selfish and self-centered.

Again, it is hard to admit that someone we love, especially when it is our parent, is selfish or self-centered. We assume that if they brought us into this world, then they must want the best for us, right? Sometimes that is the furthest thing from the truth.

Narcissists often feel entitled. They feel that everyone around them owes them something. Siblings they helped raise or they did things for should respect and admire them for their sacrifice. Their children should adore them and be at their beck and call because they birthed and raised them. Love partners should adore them and put them first often before their own children!

They feel that these things should occur simply because they are who they are. They "deserve" the attention, praise, and adoration from anyone they interact with. This is why they come off as arrogant and haughty.

If they do not receive the adoration they feel they deserve then they often become angry, bitter, and use cutting, derogatory remarks to make their target seem broken, dysfunctional or crazy. They do this because Narcissists cannot be the one with the faulty thinking. **They are never wrong**. So, something has to be wrong with anyone that doesn't think they are all that and a bag of chips!

Narcissistic mothers will often use this same tactic with their daughters. If their daughter is a high achiever, then she will use the accomplishments of her child (with or without supporting her child) as a tool to gain praise and admiration from various people for herself. You may have heard her bragging on your accomplishment to others when in reality she barely told you congratulations.

If the Narcissist's daughter is an underachiever, then she may berate the child for embarrassing her or for making it seem like she is not helping her. This goes back to the underlying belief that she has to prove to others that she is a good parent. The child is rarely questioned as to why she is struggling so that appropriate help can be obtained. The Narcissists sole focus is on the fact that her child's failure makes her "look bad" amongst her friends, peers, and family.

In some cases, the Narcissistic mother will turn their child's failure into a feature they can use to show how dedicated a mother she is to her struggling child. This occurrence has tones of Munchausen Syndrome in which the parent makes the child sicker or worse off academically in order to gain attention from doctors, school officials, etc.

The attention is still on the mother because she is so concerned and attentive towards her "broken child". No matter what, the focus is on the Narcissistic mother whether it is positive attention or negative attention.

With that said, to gauge the self-centered mind of a Narcissistic mother, just listen to her conversation. Without fail, no the matter the topic, the Narcissistic mother will turn everything around to herself. If you listen carefully, the words "I" or "Me" will consume almost 99% of her sentences! For example, if you broke your foot recently, the Narcissistic mother will begin discussing the time that she broke her foot and how painful that time was for her. So much so, that she will usually go off on a tangent about herself, her life, or some recent event that she wanted to remember to tell you.

Before you know it, you have talked with her over an hour and not one minute of that time was about you or your broken foot!

Other selfish or self-centered tactics that the Narcissistic mother may employ is giving her daughter hand-me-down items while she takes the newer items for herself. She may also withhold money or gifts given to her for the child to do things she would like to do with the money or gift.

Now that we are more aware of how to identify a Narcissistic mother, let me warn you that Narcissists have gotten smarter and wiser. They are evolving to hide in plain sight. They have picked up the skills of "acting as if" they are the most concerned and caring person in the world. However, **trust your gut because your gut never lies.**

Ask yourself what the **INTENTION** is behind the Narcissist's words and actions and the truth will reveal itself. If they have nothing to gain from helping you then maybe it is sincere and they aren't a Narcissist. However, if they get bragging rights, complaining rights, or they get to hold it over your head to blackmail you into doing whatever they say, then you are probably dealing with a Narcissist.

Understand that at the end of the day, it really is not about you. Even when they complain, this is often "secret bragging" about how much they do/ did for you. Your best defense is to remember that the **INTENTION** is the keep the limelight on them, not you.

So, what did being raised by a selfish, self-centered, Narcissistic mother teach you? It taught you that you didn't deserve the best and that hand-me-downs were "good enough." It also most likely taught you to hunger for some attention to the point of being called needy in your relationships or it taught you to deny your needs since they were never important. This develops the mindset that since your needs are unimportant then other people's needs must be more important than yours. Starting to see the picture developing? Let's keep going.

2.3 Jealous and Possessive

This is a tough one. **Your Narcissistic mother may have been or be jealous of you.** Yes, you read that correctly.

Since Narcissists believe that they are so special and unique it is hard for them to see someone else being lauded for their accomplishments, beauty, or dynamic attributes. This becomes even more apparent when they try to take credit for the accomplishments of their child. If an astute observer that is paying attention to this dynamic, refocuses the attention back on the child, then watch out. Whew! All hell might break loose!

Narcissists often feel jealous of others but they tend to turn it around and say that the person is jealous of them. A Narcissistic mother may criticize your clothing, body type, hair, accomplishments or whatever in an effort to "bring you down a notch." Here is an example: You may have gotten all A's and one B but their focus will be on that one B.

They may say that they focused on the one B because they want you to be the best and they know you can do better. That is not the whole truth. **They want you to feel that you are not quite good enough in their eyes.** They want you to stay in that position because it is under them in an approval-seeking position. This feeds their ego.

They can also be very possessive. They will verbally tear down other people that their child admires or loves in order to reign supreme in their eyes. **No one can be better than them.** So they will attempt to outperform girlfriends or boyfriends in an effort to show that no one will love you like I love you.

If their child chooses their partner against the advice of their Narcissistic mother then they will also bear the wrath of her rage.

They may be cursed out, disowned or stonewalled (refuse to talk to them) until they break up with the person. Even if they break up with the person, they will have to work to appease their mother's bruised ego in some over-the-top gestures to win back her affection.

The Narcissistic mother's goal is to control you. Her aim is to control how you think, what you do, what you say, and how you feel. They employ these tactics early in life to allow it to take root into adulthood.

To fully gauge whether or not you are dealing with a jealous/possessive, Narcissistic mother answer these questions. How does she behave when you are the center of attention? Does she do something or say something to get the attention on her while you fall back or blend into the crowd?

Has she ever picked out the worst part of a situation to harp on instead of acknowledging all the other good things that occurred in that same situation? Does she ignore you, refuse to talk with you or berate you when you choose to do something that is contrary to what she wanted you to do even if it was the best decision for you?

So what did this teach you as a child? It taught you that your mother owned you, your thoughts, your actions, your accomplishments, and your failures. It taught you that you were not good enough to ever fully please her. It taught you that what you accomplished did not really matter because she would steal the spotlight with her over-the-top antics even if it was disguised as applauding your accomplishments. It taught you that her way is the right way and your decision-making skills were faulty and not to be trusted. It taught you to not trust your own judgment.

Please Note: We are getting deep now and you may feel a little triggered. Take some time, breathe, cry, or do whatever you need to do to take care of yourself at this time. When you are ready, start again. I promise some solutions are coming but we have to pull out all the dirty laundry first to make sure that we don't miss anything during this deep soul cleaning.

2.4   Master Manipulators

Whew, chile! As my grandmother would say. This is a monster trait right her! Narcissistic mothers are master manipulators. They are very skilled at using various tactics to get you to ultimately do what they want you to do. I have taken the liberty to highlight some examples of tactics they use to manipulate you and to get you to do their bidding.

1. **Guilt Trip-** If a Narcissistic mother asks you or expects you to do something and you work up the nerve to say the forbidden word, "NO", then you can expect a guilt trip. She will most likely bring up all the things she has done for you or the sacrifices she made to get you to where you are today (real or imagined) and be flabbergasted that you will not do what she tells you to do. She may lay it on so thick that she starts to cry because of the hurt she feels. She may call you several times to express how she simply cannot believe that you were not there for her or could not do this simple task. She may be so persistent that she starts to make you regret the day you were born because you are such an ungrateful child. Even if you give in and drop everything you had planned or needed to do in order to complete

the requested task, she will hold this over your head every time she needs you do to something else. Again, it is all about control and making you feel less than. How dare you not bow down to the Queen!

2. **Comparison** – Your Narcissistic mother may compare you to siblings, other members of the family or your friends. The infamous question is often, "Why can't you be more like ___?" This is yet another tactic to make you feel not good enough by her standards. This applies even if you have accomplished ten times as much as she or the person she is comparing you too ever has in their lifetime. **Someone is always better than you**. Again, this is to keep you off kilter and feeling unworthy and not good enough.

3. **Blaming-** A Narcissistic mother will often blame you for everything going wrong in her life. She may have made you believe that if she did not have to take care of you then she would have more money. If you weren't around then she could have more of a life but instead she has to be home with you. Narcissistic mothers will blame you for their mistakes and failures because they simply cannot be wrong. Since you are in the wrong, then you must right the situation. **To do this, you must be obedient without question**. In reality, no matter how obedient you are you will still be the one to blame when things go wrong. This often takes the form of verbal abuse or physical abuse while growing up. Many Narcissistic mothers use their children as personal punching bags to allay their

anger with other people.

4. **Shaming-** A Narcissistic mother may shame their child in order to make them feel less than or not good enough. The Narcissistic mother may say that any actions that go against what they believe is right has embarrassed them or brought shame to the family. This is another tactic to control you and your actions. In order to fight for that allusive approval from your Narcissistic mother, then you must redeem yourself. Unfortunately, you will never be able to do that which will cause a perpetual cycle of you jumping through hoops to gain the approval that will never come. Some of my clients have realized that this situation has gotten so out of hand that they are basically paying for their mother to be around them.

In other words, they have to buy things for their mother in order to get her to spend time with them.

5. **Extreme Pressure-** A Narcissistic mother may put undue pressure on her child. As I mentioned in my previous example, you may have received all A's and one B in school and she will treat the B as if it were an F. She probably demanded that you perform in such a way that may not have been humanly possible. Then when you could not obtain that level of excellence, your mother may have battered your self-esteem with a verbal assault and/or physical abuse.

We will discuss ways that you can cope with or overcome the effects of having a Narcissistic mother in the Blindspot Blueprint chapter.

Vignettes:

The Narcissistic Mother

Vignette #1

Christina is a 32-year-old woman that is still afraid to disagree with her mother. As an only child, she was held under the strict scrutiny of her mother. Her mother had visions of her being her living doll. As a child, she had no choice but to dress in princess dresses and to take ballet, tap, piano lessons and anything else her mother felt would help her turn into a beautiful cultured woman.

The only problem is that Christina never wanted to do any of those things and subsequently was average at best at any of them. Her mother expressed her disappointment and embarrassment almost daily. This made Christina feel like a failure in the eyes of her mother.

When Christina left for college she disconnected with her mother unless it was time for her to go home for a visit. **For the first time she began to listen to her own voice and honor her own thoughts**. She realizes she has grown immensely but she had one obstacle to overcome. She must tell her mother no when she doesn't want to do something especially when it is highly inconvenient like having her run errands on her only day off.

Christina chose to start therapy to help her overcome her "mommy issues". She learned that she had been manipulated her entire life! She had been made to feel bad or wrong when she disagreed with her mother's plans. In reality, she wasn't wrong. She wasn't bad because she had interests that were different from her mother's interests.

After months of therapy, Christina finally uttered the word, NO. It was quiet and soft. Her mother even asked her to repeat what she said. She repeated it. Her natural urge was to give an excuse but she didn't. Her mother immediately started in about all she had sacrificed for her and yet she told her no. Christina stuck to her guns and did not recant what she said. Her mother slammed the phone down in her face. This hurt Christina but she resisted the urge to call her back and try to make it all better. She was not being mean. She was simply honoring herself and that felt good.

Vignette #2

Taylor is a 50-year-old woman. She is married with three grown children and she is struggling. She is not struggling financially but emotionally.

She is sitting on the couch in a counseling office describing her life as a house of cards have finally fallen down and she doesn't know how to put all the pieces back together again. For so long, she has overlooked the volatile nature of her relationship with her mother but she is tired of overlooking her "flaws" and allowing herself to knowingly be mistreated. She doesn't believe that her mother ever loved her or that she even likes her.

Fighting back the tears, she recalls her childhood. Several of her mother's boyfriends raped her from the age of 5 years to 10 years of age. She believes her mother knew and either accepted money for it or pretended not to notice.

Taylor keeps asking, mostly to herself, how do you not notice your boyfriend being missing in the middle of the night for over 20-30 minutes? It sickens her to think that her mother knew and allowed it to take place.

Along with the sexual abuse, she recounts episodes of extreme verbal and physical abuse at the hands of her mother. Her mother called her every curse word in the book and reminded her daily that she wasn't ever gonna be shit. She constantly told her that even her father did not want her. Finally, when she was 10 years old a friend's family took her in.

She thrived there and didn't realize how hungry for love and attention she really was. Thankfully, her friend's mother was loving and provided a safe place for her to grow up and finish school. Her mother never checked on her or sent money to help out.

Taylor figured that it was due to her newest boyfriend or the obsessive relationship she had with her son.

After months of EMDR, to reprocess the traumatic memories within her childhood, we were finally in a position to talk about finding closure with her mother. Taylor didn't want to talk to her mother. She said that she hated her and then recanted in a ball of emotion and tears. She admitted that she didn't hate her but simply wanted her to love her. The lack of love she did not receive from her mother helped to make her susceptible to violent and abusive men. She didn't think she deserved better. Her mother's words had become a self-fulfilling prophecy even though she exceled in school and subsequently her career. Taylor admitted that she did well with things she could control but humans were another issue.

She stated that she felt more comfortable with animals than humans because they did not seek to hurt you but only to love you.

After some time, Taylor made the decision to write her mother a letter to finally speak her truth. She said it was the hardest thing she ever did but not being beaten down verbally or physically for speaking her truth felt good. She is making steady progress and working hard to release the other negative people out of her life. She doesn't believe she will ever speak to her mother again and calls her toxic. However, she is working hard to move forward into a vision that she foresees for herself.

Chapter 3:

Perfectionism

Perfectionism is not a mental disorder. However, it is more of a type of behavior that can put a person at risk for developing a mental disorder.

Perfectionistic behaviors usually start from an outside influence (i.e. parent, coach, etc.) and becomes internalized within the person. Research has shown that parental influence is a big indicator as to whether or not a person will develop Perfectionistic traits. Once these traits have been ingrained in a person throughout their childhood, the person often becomes even harder on themselves than their parents ever were!

It also doesn't help that in our society, Perfectionistic tendencies tend to be applauded and looked fondly upon. Everyone wants to strive for perfection. Everyone wants to be the best.

The psychological effects of perfectionism range from anxiety and depression to more serious psychological mental disorders. It is considered to be a risk factor for many other mental disorders such as obsessive-compulsive disorder, eating disorders, anxiety disorders, phobias, substance abuse use and much more! The pressure to succeed and to be better than the rest can often cause individuals to overexert themselves to the point of physical exhaustion or mental breakdown. This "competitive edge" of being the absolute best in your endeavors is said to separate the men from the boys, but at what cost?

Let's dive in into the different aspects of Perfectionism and how this may be contributing to your feelings of burn-out.

3.1 Excessive Concern Over Mistakes

If you have an excessive concern over your mistakes, then you probably cannot let it go if you fail at something or do not perform your absolute best. You may feel that you know what your best is and even if you win the competition, get the job, or passed the class with an A, you still may feel that you did not give it your all.

You may continue to beat yourself up long after the situation has passed and have feelings of not being good enough or of being unjustified in receiving the award, trophy, acknowledgement, etc. that you received.

The self-punishment is even worse when you do actually fail at something.

As a Perfectionist, you tend to perform very well in situations that you can control like work or school. However, you may struggle with your interactions with people. This is because you cannot control another human being's feelings and/or thoughts. So, when a person does not behave the way that they "should", then most likely you internalize the errors, tell yourself that it is your fault, and then start blaming yourself for the "failure of the relationship" or the mistakes. Totally omitting the fact that you were not in a relationship alone and your partner needs to take ownership of what he or she did to make the relationship fail.

This type of behavior often originates as a result of having a Narcissistic mother.

If you were harshly disciplined or verbally attacked due to any small or large mistake that you made, then you learned that it was not ok to make a mistake. You had to be good at everything, all the time, without fail or you yourself were a failure.

After fearfully trying something for the first time, possibly not excelling at it, and then receiving a poor grade, score, etc. to only be verbally abused and/or physically abused when you presented the information to your Narcissistic mother, you were groomed to beat yourself up when you did not do a "perfect" job. Since "perfect" does not really exist, then it was impossible for you to ever be good enough.

Let me say that again, the setup was that "perfect" doesn't exist. It is subjective to the person that is judging the situation.

This is why some people may see getting all A's and one B as exemplary and spectacular, while others may see it as subpar and average. It depends on the barometer of the person measuring the outcome.

News Flash! Who would have thought that this scale, measurement, or barometer that you use to measure everything you do was all in your head? You control the dial. So, if you can turn it up as far as it can go to 100 then you can also turn it down to 0. Or you can gauge the situation and move it accordingly.

So hear me when I say that you do not have to be on 100 everyday, sweetheart. If you have the flu and you are weak, nauseous, and experiencing malaise then your best may be to get out the bed to shower for the day.

When you are healthy, happy, and in good spirits, your best might be at a full 100. It's all up to you since you control the dial.

I often ask my clients to tell themselves that they are only one person and that they are doing the best that they can at the moment. To me, that is giving yourself grace to be human and to be flawed. Flawed is what makes us unique and relatable. We all know that no one, and I mean no one, has lived an absolutely perfect life. Some come close but some type of tragedy, illness, or slump has occurred in their life at some time.

So, stop thinking that you will ever attain Perfection because you won't. Not ever. Give it your best and then let it go.

3.2 Excessively High Personal Standards

If you had a Narcissistic mother then you were told that you had to be the best at all times. There were no days off. You had to be "Perfect" at all times and with everything you did.

This mean that how you looked had to be on point even when you were relaxing at home, your skin and body had to be flawless, your cleaning habits, schoolwork, friends, hobbies, and all other interactions had to fall in line with the perfect vision she had for you growing up.

If for some "strange" reason, there was a flaw such as you not cleaning up "correctly", you got a blemish on your face, you did not perform well at your last recital, you were hurt by a boy you like, or your friends were not as perfect as you thought they were then they had to go and you were most likely berated for the flaw endlessly.

This taught you that you had to be better than everyone else all the time. Even if you kept that thought inside, it may have been hard for you to establish real friendships because they could most likely feel that you were secretly competing with them. If not, they may have felt that you thought they were not on your level and no competition, so they were safe. What kind of friend is that? This is where competition often begins with women. Many women have been groomed to compete and/or to not trust other women by their own mother.

When you have excessively high personal standards you are always on.

Nothing can survive being on 24/7. Lights blow, cars stop working, and people burn-out when you do this. It is like running a car endlessly at 100 mph. Nothing can sustain this long-term. Nothing. Including you.

It's time to stop running your life at 100 mph. Stop, take the cape off, and explore what simply being your flawed self actually looks and feels like. The good part is despite the brainwashing you may have experienced as a child that has gotten you to this point, you are no longer a child. You can start today making decisions for your good.

We will discuss ways to deal with Perfectionism in the Blindspot Blueprint chapter.

3.3 High Parental Expectations

I won't belabor this point because you just read a whole chapter on the Narcissistic mother. However, I have faith in you that by now you understand how detrimental it was to your psyche to be held to an unattainable standard as a child.

It is quite normal for parents to want the best for their children. I think that all "healthy" parents want their kids to grow up to be better than them and to live a more successful life than they did. However, when there is little to no concern about how the child feels about taking on six hobbies that they do not like and being expected to perform well in each of them or they are forced to be in pageants or other things that do not suit their personality type, it becomes a form of mental torture.

This is why as an adult you may struggle with trusting your own decisions and figuring out what is best for you since you never had practice doing that.

3.4 Parental Criticism

Again, I won't belabor this point either due to the last chapter. However, I will stress the point that parental criticism is the equivalent of mental torture.

All children start off simply wanting their parent to love, nurture and praise them. This is how they figure out when they are performing well or performing poorly. It is the responsibility of the parent to let the child know what they are doing right and wrong.

However, when you are dealing with a Narcissistic mother, this process is warped.

As a child, you may have never heard anything positive about the things you did well or you may have received a dry, "That's good." When you did not perform well or there was some slight imperfection that your Narcissistic mother's trained eyes could catch, then you were probably battered over the head with it endlessly. In other words, she may have harped on the bad and ignored the good. It probably felt almost as if you were in an alternate universe. The bad was celebrated and the good was basically ignored. This type of behavior would affect anyone.

As a child you may have felt like a trick pony, trying to appease your mother by showing her how high and how fast you could run and jump through her hoops even to the point of mental and physical exhaustion.

Even when being rightfully exhausted, you may have found some drops of strength to crawl through one last hoop hoping for just a drop of her praise and/or love. Again to no avail.

As heartbreaking as this realization is it is important that you realize that today we are starting over. Today, as you read this book and gain perspective, I want you to realize that things are changing.

Of course, you know I'll have more information on what you can do to continue this process of change in the Blindspot Blueprint chapter.

3.5 Exaggerated Emphasis On Precision

If you are a Perfectionist then you most likely fixate on precision. You may have been a child that was taught that it was against the law to color outside the lines, so you never wavered!

This is an exaggeration but it may have felt like it was that serious when you were growing up. Nothing could be flawed or there would be a natural consequence to soon follow.

That most likely created a fear-based thinking pattern in you. This fear-based thinking kept you in line and most importantly under your mother's control. Although, it also may have backfired as you entered adulthood.

You most likely have been so controlled that now you may have created a self-imposed prison to keep yourself in line and out of trouble. This means that there is little variance on how you do things. Once you have come up with your perfect pattern of doing something it probably will never change.

This would work perfectly if you were in this world alone. Other people or even little people, called kids, come to teach us the beauty in letting go of all these self-imposed ways of doing things and to realize that if it is not done just so then it is still done. Perfectionistic thinking tends to lead to things being left undone.

An example of this is if you married someone that is not as neat as you are. You have your almost ritualistic ways of doing things but your partner does not. So, you struggle with their untidiness. The dilemma is whether or not you clean it up or let it stay for your partner to clean it up. Perfectionists struggle with that because they have been taught that everything must be perfect all the time.

However, cleaning up behind someone that is fully capable of doing it himself/herself can become frustrating and tiresome. So, what is a Perfectionist to do? I have take great pleasure in hearing a Perfectionist say I am done cleaning up behind my partner. I have decided to leave it till he or she sees it.

That is the beginning of breaking the Obsessive-Compulsive Disorder that started as a result of being groomed to be a Perfectionist. As a therapist, to see the pressure valve be released just a little is so rewarding and a major step toward a Perfectionist's healing.

We will discuss this further in the Blindspot Blueprint chapter.

3.6 Order and Organization

The Perfectionist's need for order and organization is how Obsessive-Compulsion Disorder (OCD) begins.

The Perfectionist doesn't get days off, so they are taught that they must be at peak performance no matter what they do. So, this easily gets translated to a child that everything must be perfect. Often this is the mantra that runs in the Perfectionist's brain while they do anything. It must be perfect. It must be perfect.

Since we have established that perfection does not exist, the Perfectionist has set themselves up for failure.

If you are a Perfectionist, or at least have Perfectionistic tendencies, then you must have order and organization in order for your world to make sense. Truth be told, a messy area/space can be indicative of a messy, or out of control mind. However, when a person is unable to rest if there is one dish in the sink or there is a missing vacuum line on the floor, then you are no longer dealing with cleanliness and a level of order.

You are now dealing with obsessive thoughts that will not let you rest. These thoughts constantly remind you that you will feel so much better once you wash that dish. Meanwhile, you are most likely dealing with the uncontrollable compulsion or urge to wash the dish. This is where the Obsessive-Compulsive Disorder and other Anxiety Disorders are bred and nurtured until they take over your life.

3.7 Doubts about Actions

Do you find yourself constantly asking others their opinions about what you should do in any situation? This is usually a hallmark of Perfectionism and having had a Narcissistic mother.

If you had a Narcissistic mother then she most likely made all the decisions.

You were not asked what color dress you wanted or what you wanted to eat or even what hobby you were interested in. Your opinion did not matter. You were her child/object that she had to take care of and if she had to take care of you then you did exactly what she wanted. You were not allowed to have a thought or to feel any kind of way. The only way you could feel is happy whether you liked it or not.

So, it is no wonder that you struggle with honoring and listening to your own voice. Didn't know you had a voice, did you? Why yes you do!

So, as an adult, you now have the opportunity to listen to your own voice but it most likely frightens you. It frightens you because you are scared to make a mistake.

What if you choose the wrong thing? What if what you want doesn't make sense? Perfectionists will often call themselves derogatory names at this point such as stupid or dumb which couldn't be further from the truth. You are just scared and it is ok.

Perfectionists also tend to rattle off the times they made a choice and it did not go well. Like that time when they liked this guy that ended up using them and dogging them out. Or that time that they trusted a friend with a secret and she went out and told everyone what she said. Perfectionists will use one or both of these examples that quite possibly happened in middle or high school as a rationale as to why they can't trust their judgment now at 50 years of age.

When you say it out loud, it may not make sense but when a person is accustomed to having failures or mistakes held over their heads by Narcissistic mothers, indefinitely, then they learn to do the same thing, if not worse, to themselves.

The truth is that we all have made mistakes and used poor judgment in who we chose to date or befriend. That does not mean we are flawed and broken. We simply judged the person's "representative" wrong and made a mistake. The key is to learn from the lesson. Not to imprison yourself into a world of isolation so that you can't be betrayed again or to ask what everyone else thinks you should do. You simply make sure you learn form that mistake. That is giving yourself grace to be human and that is essentially what this journey called life is about.

3.8 The Dark Side Of Perfectionism

I want to take a moment to talk about the dark side of Perfectionism. This is a topic that fascinates me as a therapist but it has not really been explored in research and is rarely discussed. I think it is because a lot of people don't put the two together.

To me, the dark side of Perfectionism, is the other side of the same coin. Perfectionist often look like all that I have described above. They are overachievers, highflyers, and compete with the best of them no matter the task.

On the other side of Perfectionism are the underachievers. They most likely grew up with a Narcissistic mother and possibly an overachieving sibling.

For various reasons, they decided that there is no way that they can live up to those extremely high standards of their Narcissistic mother so they won't even try. They gave up. They got tired of the shaming and the comparisons to their sibling. They decided that they will be the total opposite. So, they may have gotten involved with the illegal side of life or became very rebellious so that they could distance themselves and create their own identity outside the world of perfection.

The underachiever may not participate in hobbies, perform well in school, or attempt things that they don't feel they will succeed in. **The underachiever is often a perfectionist that has never tried.** They learned early that it is safer to not try rather than to try and fail. So they don't.

This is heartbreaking because underachievers are often brilliant people. Their fear has taught them that it is safer to hang among the bottom feeders of life rather than to excel. Excelling is hard and takes work. It also puts you "out there" because others will assess how well you are doing including your Narcissistic mother. However, if you don't try then they will never know what you can and can't do and may assume that you have untapped potential. That is a lot safer than knowing you cannot do something.

Another caveat that I want to mention is that overachieving Perfectionists often have areas in their life when they behave the exact same way.

They may excel at most things but have one area such as dancing that they refuse to even try because they fear that they will not be good at it and others may laugh. This thought pattern breeds anxiety and phobias.

Vignettes:

The Perfectionist

Vignette #3

Kimberly is a 22-year-old woman that grew up with high achieving parents. Her father is a well-known, powerful attorney and her mother is a well-respected and admired socialite in their community. Together they make the perfect couple. When they had their only child, Kimberly, she became their everything. She was their princess and angel. To her mother, her beautiful baby was her living doll.

As Kimberly aged, she grew to hate pink dresses and frills. She felt that she was more of a tomboy type and wanted to play outside, climb trees, and play with animals she read about in books.

Her father was not averse to giving her down time just to play, be rough and get dirty. However, he was rarely home.

Her mother on the other had refused to allow her to risk getting bruised and dirty which could cause her to get sick with some type of disease. Since Kimberly was more often than not with her mother, she had to do as she was told even if she hated it.

Kimberly longed to play and be like everyone else. While others were preparing for parties, hanging out with friends and liking boys, she was constantly preparing for some type of recital or performance. She felt so distant and different from other kids her age.

When Kimberly graduated high school with honors, she hoped that she could get away from her mother and attend a school of her choice. Unfortunately, her mother's plan was for her to stay local and attend her father's alma mater. Since they were paying for it, again she had no choice.

That was the theme of Kimberly's life. She had no choice. She had no control.

Bingeing and purging seemed to spiral out of control overnight. It started with her enjoying a family meal and then being criticized by her mother for eating too much knowing she was preparing for a performance. Then the comments became increasingly hurtful and rude. Her mom would call her fat or criticize the size of her butt or breasts knowing there was little she could do to change those things.

So the first time she ate a big meal, felt nauseous and decided to induce vomiting was quite haphazard. What she found was that it did make her feel so much lighter. She had eaten and enjoyed a big meal but now she could "erase it" by vomiting.

That realization turned into a full-blown eating disorder that no one seemed to notice. Her mother even applauded her on how thin she was and how her clothing fit her so well. Everyone was happy, right?

It wasn't until a pageant director brought her newfound "thinness" to the attention of her father that she was asked what was going on. She did not immediately admit to bingeing and purging but the look of concern in her father's eyes eventually broke her.

After months of care in an eating disorder facility and continued therapy after she was discharged, Kimberly is on her way to recovery.

Vignette #4

Passion is a 44-year-old woman that grew up with a Narcissistic single mother. She has an older sister that is a classic overachiever.

Passion feels that she has always lived in the shadow of her sister. Not only did her mother compare her to her sister but going through the same schools that her sister attended was also a nightmare. If she got in trouble, teachers would ask why she couldn't be more like her sister. That pissed her off more than anything. She was not her sister and she didn't want to be like Miss Goody Two Shoes. She was herself even though she was unsure as to who "herself" actually was.

She barely made it through middle school and started out on a twisted journey through high school.

No one explained to her that she had Dyslexia and that she simply saw words backwards. It wasn't that she was slow or retarded but it was simply how her brain worked. More importantly, it did not mean that she had to be a failure at life. She simply had to work a little longer to understand her assignments. There are people who have gotten doctorate degrees from Harvard that have Dyslexia so she could achieve whatever she wanted to achieve as well.

The problem is that Passion's Narcissistic mother felt that she was broken and that something was wrong with her which ultimately meant that it "appeared" that her mother did something wrong.

The fact that her father walked out on them when she was born further fueled the thought pattern in her mother that he left, not because of their relationship, but because Passion had done something wrong.

This guilt, of being the cause of everything wrong in the family, ate away at Passion. She felt hurt that her mother blamed her for everything but that hurt soon turned into unexpressed rage. She decided that if she as already a failure at life then she would ride that bus until the wheels came off.

She dropped out of high school and started hanging with the goth crowd. She did work but could be seen panhandling around town. Eventually, the band of "misfits" hitchhiked to different cities.

She lost contact with her mother and sister which is exactly what she wanted to do. She wasn't shit and she wasn't going to be shit.

This mindset lead to abusive relationships and run-ins with the law. She was often arrested for stealing and eventually prostitution. To deal with all the mental anguish and reminders of how she had "failed" at life, she turned to drugs. There was blessed relief in the drugs because she didn't have to feel or remember...anything.

After overdosing several times, she was put into a drug rehab center. There she got her life back. She was 44 years old and felt like she finally had a purpose. She now counsels other women that have had their life derailed by drugs and violence. She has found her perfect purpose.

Chapter 4:

Codependency

We hear the word Codependency tossed around a lot these days. However, the true scope of what Codependency entails is often not fully understood.

Codependency in its simplest form is the act of helping- on steroids. It occurs when your good intentions becomes the tool that manipulators use to take from you until you have nothing else to give.

Codependency is a relationship of sorts. It must involve at least two people. **It is an unhealthy attachment to another person**. The roots of Codependency are grounded in addiction therapy. Either you are the Enabler or the Enabled. Addicts are often the enabled ones that rely on others to take care of them or to help them. The Enabler is the one that provides the Enabled person a safe place to fall and enjoy their addiction.

Now, we are seeing this dynamic in non-addiction related relationships. It can occur in Narcissistic parenting relationships as well as in love relationships that include an intimate partner, family member or friend. Any time there is overcompensation of one person to help another person or persons with little to no reciprocity then it is a Codependent situation.

Also, in Codependent situations or relationships, you are not allowed to be weak, tired, scared, depressed or anything besides ready for action. This is because they view you as their rock. You are their stability. If you give up, then the enabled person fears that they will not be able to make it because they rely on you so much. This is a very unhealthy dynamic.

So, how do you know that you are in a Codependent situation or relationship? Keep reading.

4.1 They Take and You Give

Takers, or let's be honest- Users, are often self-centered and selfish. Sound familiar? Like Narcissistic mother's they feel entitled and they believe that people should help them. The justifications can vary. You are their daughter, sister, wife or mother so you owe them.

What you owe them varies on what you can offer. If you have a great job and money to offer, then they will always have a bill that they need you to pay for them. If you have a new vehicle, then you need to take them to their appointments or to the store whenever they call. If you have a nice home with lots of room, they should be able to stay with you. If you have a flexible schedule, then you should run them around on your days off. You get the picture. Whatever you have they want it, need it and deserve it.

With that said, they will never be able to repay the favor. If you need them to watch your kids, they will be too busy or have a headache. If you need money, or your money back, then they didn't make enough this last payday or yet another issue has surfaced and requires their money. Again, you get the picture. You will always, always be the one giving and they will always be the one taking.

The saddest part of this is that takers have no limit or boundaries. They will forever need your help or your resources. I often use the example that you could be laying on the floor with your last drop of blood in your vein and they will take that because in a few minutes you won't be needing it anyway!

It is an unquenching need and sense of entitlement to you and your things.

4.2 No Benefit To You

People that have grown up with the idea that they don't matter have very low self-worth and yet these are the very people that will give their last dime to others. They tend to do this simply because in their "subconscious mind" they hope that one day that person or someone will reciprocate. In their conscious mind and even out loud, an enabler may say that they do things for others because they would want someone to do that for them if they needed it.

That is an admirable trait and it comes from a pure heart but at the end of the day that will never happen. Perfectionists rarely ask for help because it makes them look as if they can't handle their situation. The person that they are doing these things for will most likely never offer or even ask if they need anything because they are takers or users. So the dynamic is perpetual.

The problem is that Perfectionists get so caught up in proving how much they can be there for someone else that they forget to stop and assess how much the person they are helping is actually there for them which is usually not at all. They may be nice to them, tell them that they love them, or spend some time with them while they are getting what they want but as soon as they have obtained what they want they are out of there.

So, I often ask my clients that are in a Codependent situation, "What is the benefit for you?" There is usually a long pause as they try to come up with something. Usually it is nothing remotely on the level that they are giving. Then slowly the realization starts to dawn on them. They were essentially paying to have a mom, or paying to have a relationship, or paying to have some sense of family.

They may have paid with their money, time, energy or material possessions but at the end of the day they paid something.

The other realization that comes as we continue therapy is that all of their efforts does not benefit them and it is not benefitting the person they are enabling either. The drug addict is still enjoying their drugs at the detriment of their future and their family. The money issues that you mother has every month still exist every month. They often get worse because she knows you will bail her out so she has even more fun with her paychecks. Your boyfriend's car will never get fixed because he can take yours all day and he knows you will definitely keep your car up and running. On and on. At the end of the day, no one wins.

Seems hopeless but its not. Just hold on because I will dive into this topic in the Blindspot Blueprint chapter.

4.3 Resentment and Guilt

A foolproof sign that you are in a Codependent situation or relationship is that you feel both resentful and guilty about helping the person you are enabling. You give and give and give and the situation does not get better, it only gets worse. So you get tired of giving but there is always something that you need to do for this person. This can cause anyone to become resentful. You technically are caught in a loop of doing things against your will. Your kindness has just become your weakness. You know that you are being used but you don't know how to stop it.

I could easily say to just tell them no and that will stop it but then the guilt will enter the picture. If you tell them no then what will happen to their lights, their phone, their kids, or even their job?

You MUST do this thing to save them or they will fail, falter, or do something to jeopardize their future. To a Perfectionist this is unheard of so they don their cape and do the thing they don't feel like doing which only breeds more resentment and the cycle continues.

All the while, the enabled person gets the benefit of not having to be accountable, not growing up and not having to be responsible for their own life and decisions because they know you will come in and save the day.

Harboring these often-unexpressed feelings of resentment tend to make a person sick. Blood pressure soars, anxiety takes hold, and many other psychological symptoms begin to present themselves because emotionally and mentally you are out of order. You are stuck in a loop of dysfunction. This will eventually show up physically to get your attention.

Vignettes:

Codependency

Vignette #5

Christian is a 35-year-old woman with two kids, a husband, a close-knit family and she is tired. Christian works a full-time job and is very active in her children's afterschool activities. She tries her best to be attentive to her husband and plans date nights to keep the romance alive. Christian also participates on the church choir, is a homeroom mom for both of her kids and she teaches a body pump class at 5 am every Wednesday.

Christian loves her family and feels that she has a good relationship with all of them. She prides herself in planning all the family Christmas events because they are generally at her house. Christian has one sister that is struggling. She is an on and off again crack user. Christian doesn't know why she turned to crack but she has seen her sister's steady decline.

All of Christian's life she has been the reliable big sister. Her sister always seemed to be more fragile. Christian recalls fighting neighborhood girls that would bully her sister. She also remembers taking the blame for stuff her sister did so that she would not get the spanking. She cannot recall why she felt she had to be so protective of her sister. She just always has.

Her sister is only one year younger than she is but she acts like she is stuck in her teens. She parties almost everyday which opened the door for her crack habit. Her last boyfriend was very abusive and yet she refused to leave him. They separated only because he went to jail for robbery. Now, her sister tells her that she doesn't know how she will cope without him. She feels that she has been left behind to care for her two young children alone.

This breaks Christian's heart. She loves her two nieces and refuses to see them go down the drain with her sister. So, she visits her sister's house daily to make sure that it is clean, that the kids have eaten, and that all the utilities are still working. She gives her sister money almost daily because she always has something that is due or that she needs for the kids. Truthfully, Christian knows it is just to feed her habit but she doesn't know how to stop it. If she doesn't give it to her, she fears her sister may prostitute herself or something worse to get the money.

Her relationship with her sister has taken such a toll on her that she has started to not sleep at night. She often sneaks out the house to ride by her sister's house to make sure her sister's car is there. She convinces herself that if she is there then the kids are safe.

She then goes home and tries to get back to sleep before she has to go to the gym in two hours.

She knows that this has to stop and even her mother has told her to stop. Friends and her husband have told her that she can't want more for her sister than her sister wants for herself but she can't seem to let go. She can't risk the kids being in that cold house, with no food, and dirty diapers.

She has asked her sister to give the kids to her and her sister refuses. She didn't even asked her husband before she blurted it out. She just knows that something needs to be done. She doesn't want to call social services and get her sister in trouble. However, her hair is starting to fall out, she has constant headaches, and she has lost 20 lbs. that she wasn't trying to lose. She feels like she is at her wits end but doesn't know how to make the train stop.

So, she decided to seek counseling to at least get an objective opinion about her situation. Since starting therapy, Christian has really been thinking about when this Codependency thing started. She feels like she was the target of her mother's criticism and wrath when she did something wrong. She didn't like it at all but she felt she could take it. Her sister on the other hand didn't seem to be so strong. She would literally shut down and become almost mute when her mother would yell at, punish, or spank her. Christian feels that seeing that made her take on her sister's punishment as well as her own. The only thing is she is tired. She is always there for her sister but her sister never asks her how she is feeling or if she is ok. As a matter of fact, no one asks her how she feels and if she is ok. It is assumed that she always is but she is realizing that she really isn't. She is not ok and it is time for a change.

Vignette #6

August is 41 years old and feels she is emotionally damaged. She decided to come to counseling to work through some deeply buried traumas that she is ready to work through. She feels that she goes through life looking at it from the outside. If someone asks her to do something she does it even if she doesn't want to. If someone wants free, unattached, and unprotected sex, she feels almost required to do it. She cant's say no to anyone or anything and she doesn't quite understand why.

August began our sessions by discussing more mundane things that happened to her that hurt her as a child. Having her childhood best friend move away was quietly devastating to her.

August has learned in therapy that there are **Big T traumas** such as murders, rapes, suicides, etc.

These events change your life forever and the average onlooker can see that the person that witnessed this will be changed forever. Then there are **Small t traumas** such as molestations, losing a job, or having your heart broken. Those things are just as painful and change your life forever but somehow you are able to keep moving forward the next day despite feeling broken.

August learned that her best friend moving away was a Small t trauma but it was a trauma that needed to be processed. After we worked on that trauma, August slowly but surely began to dig deeper. She realized that the things that happened to her were not her fault and she no longer needed to protect the perpetrators that raped and molested her. She uttered secrets in therapy that she had never told anyone and that will never be shared with anyone.

Slowly and unbeknownst to August she began to find her voice. She began to see that she was not broken or wrong. She had survived a Narcissistic mother, sexually sadistic people that used her body and then discarded it, and she survived creating her own torment with the men that she allowed to do the same to her with her consent.

She went into some very dark and scary places within herself and came out bruised but not broken.

Her journey continues....

Chapter 5:

The Blindspot

Blueprint

Congratulations! You made it through! I hope that the examples and the stories I shared with you helped you to understand why you may be feeling burned-out.

In each of the chapters, I referred to the Blueprint at the end of the book. This Blueprint will provide you with the overall diagnosis, the symptoms you should be on the lookout for and most importantly the interventions or things you can do to work on or completely eradicate these issues.

I'm excited for you! Let's begin….

The Blindspot Blueprint: The Narcissistic Mother

Diagnosis: Narcissistic Mother

Diagnostic Criteria:

1. She is Emotionally Distant.

2. She is Selfish and Self-Centered

3. She is Jealous and Possessive

4. She is a Master Manipulator

Interventions:

1. **Awareness**- I always teach my clients that the first step to any change is to become aware that there is even a problem. If your mother or anyone else for that matter makes you feel worse around them than when you are not around them then there is a problem. You can journal about your thoughts or you can find a close friend to talk to but know that it is time to take the blinders off

and see her for who she really is and what she really did to you as a child and as an adult.

2. **<u>Accept and Allow</u>**: Narcissists rarely change and when they do change it is usually small, baby steps after many years. If your mother does not see herself as wrong then the likelihood of her changing is little to none. So, it is time for you to accept who she is without sugarcoating it. You must accept her for who she is, flaws and all, and allow it to be so.

3. **<u>Mourn</u>**: The little girl in you needs to mourn the fact that your mother will never be who you **<u>need</u>** her to be. She is your mother and she may have done the very best she could have done…or not. Either way, the past is the past and you can't change it.

You have to let your little girl heart break and realize that your mother will never be the supportive, nurturing, loving, and attentive mother you needed her to be. She is who she is and it's time to accept that. Let your heart break. I promise that you wont cry forever. If you really struggle with this then I would suggest seeing a therapist to go on that painful journey with you.

4. **<u>Work on Yourself</u>**: When people are recovering from Narcissistic parenting, it is so important to discover who you are and not who others say you are. You have to take the time to find your own voice. You do that by disentangling your voice from your mother's voice.

We all have three voices playing in our head at any time. It is either your **Parent's voice** telling you what to do and what is right and what is wrong. If your parent's voice was critical of you then you will hear those negative comments as well. We also have an **Adult voice** This is our inner voice that tells us to do the responsible thing like go to bed early, go to work, pick the kids up from school. The last voice gets ignored so much! That is the **Child's voice**. She is still in there and would love to come out and play. She is the one that remembers all the childhood things that could include verbal abuse, physical abuse, sexual abuse, mental and emotional abuse that occurred in your childhood. When you say that you have pushed those thoughts and memories down…well she is the one that holds on to them for you so that you can get on with your day. When you face her, apologize to her for being as hurtful to her as others were and for neglecting her when you pushed her down, she begins to heal. She begins to feel it is safe to come out to play and to simply be a kid. So, listen to her sometimes. Ask her what she wants to do today. I bet she will answer! It will probably be something you like to do but have refused to allow yourself to do like coloring, getting ice cream, writing, watching cartoons, or going to a playground.

5. **Seek Help**: If this process is too much for you to handle do not hesitate to seek help from a therapist. We are trained to hold space for you.

What that means is we are strong enough and knowledgeable enough to go into the depths of your hell with you so that you don't have to do it alone. While we are there, we point out things that may be in your blindspot. No judgment. Just noticing. This is what we are trained to do. There is no shame in reaching out for help. Even if you have to go in "secret", just go.

The Blindspot Blueprint: Perfectionism

Diagnosis: Perfectionism

Diagnostic Criteria:

1. Excessive Concern Over Mistakes
2. Excessively High Personal Standards
3. High Parental Expectations
4. High Parental Criticism
5. Exaggerated Emphasis on Precision
6. Order and Organization
7. Doubts About Actions
8. The Dark Side Of Perfectionism

Interventions:

6. **Awareness**- Awareness is the first step to solving any problem. If you are unaware of what is happening to you then you are in a state of mindlessness. The first course of action is to become mindful. Pay attention. Take notes. Become aware of your surroundings and the people in it.

Then write down or evaluate what you see. Do you see yourself behaving in any of the ways listed above?

7. **Acknowledge**- Once you are aware that a problem exists then you need to acknowledge it. Get as clear as possible about what your perfectionistic traits are and where they originated from. This is not about the blame game but about being honest about where you learned to be so hard on yourself. Who first told you that you were useless, a failure, or dumb? Clients are always shocked when I ask that because the thought usually did not start from them but someone told them or someone put excessive pressure on them to be perfect. Who was that person? Give them back that negativity and stop taking ownership of someone else's stuff.

8. **Erase The Script**- You have been brainwashed. Yes it does exist and not only in prisoner of war scenarios. Brainwashing is still alive and well today in the homes of many Narcissists. Think about it. If babies are what we call, Tabula Rasa or blank slates, who are the first people to write something on the slate? Your parents, family members and siblings. So, if they were in a toxic, dysfunctional state then like or not, so were you. You learned to view the world through their eyes. What your parent(s) said was the gospel truth. Why wouldn't it be? It was all you knew!

So, if their truth is wrong or faulty then your truth is wrong or faulty. So, a major part of overcoming Perfectionism is taking the time to erase the script.

You have to dive in with a qualified therapist or at the least a pen and paper and decipher those irrational thoughts. Who are you without someone telling you who you are? Listen to no other voice but your own. **Who are you?** The answer may shock you. Erase the old script and replace it with new information in your own voice.

9. **<u>Fight Back</u>**- It is time to fight for...YOU! You do not have to willingly accept those irrational, negative thoughts that come to you in everyone else's voice but your own. You can't stop them from coming but when they come you can be ready to fight! What are those negative things that you tell yourself when you make a mistake or don't know how to do something?

Make a note of them and then make a note of the things you didn't know how to do but you did them anyway and exceled. Or write down those things that you did and failed at it the first time. Did you enjoy the process and did you learn something from it? Then it was worth the effort. This new way of thinking is the key you need to open the chains of fear that have kept you in a safe box all of your life.

The Blindspot Blueprint: Codependency

Diagnosis: Codependency

Diagnostic Criteria:

1. They Take and You Give
2. No Benefit To You
3. Resentment and Guilt

Interventions:

10. **Awareness**- For the last time, I have to start with awareness. As I said in the Codependency chapter, people get so busy giving and giving to others that they rarely take the time to stop, look around, and notice who is giving to you. It's time to look around. Take notes while you're at it. I'll wait. Finished already? Let's move to my next point.

11. **They Have To Be Responsible For Themselves**- I know I will have to give you a moment to let that one soak in because it is a big one!

Grownups, people over the age of 18 years of age, have to be responsible for themselves. This is their life and they know right from wrong just like you do. They are making a CHOICE to do wrong. I can hear someone say, "But what if they are on drugs, is that their choice?" My answer is YES! They learned about drugs just like you did in school. They have seen the horrible effects of drugs. If it is not drugs, then they knew that that same bill would be due the same time each month, so why spend your money on shoes? They know that their kids will need diapers and milk, so why go party and blow your whole check? The answer is simple. They made a CHOICE. So, since they are making a CHOICE to do things that keep them in jeopardy and in NEED, then you have the right to make a different

CHOICE and say no the next time they ask you for something. Hello? You still there? I hear crickets....

12. **<u>Set Boundaries:</u>** If you are in a Codependent situation, not only do you have to realize that the person you are ENABLING is responsible for him or herself, but you also have to begin the process of working on your BOUNDARIES. I like to call it the BIG B WORD- Boundaries. It takes work and a whole lot of emotions to work through but you can do it. You can figure out what your NON-NEGOTIBLES are. Those non-negotiables are those things that you simply will not do. It is a line that you refuse to cross anymore. An extreme example of this is if you decide that if any man puts his hands on you then you are out of there, the first time.

That is a firm NON-NEGOTIABLE or BOUNDARY. The key here is that it is not enough to talk bad and sound good, you have to be at a point where you are willing to back it up come hell or high water. No matter how much you love someone, you have to get to a point that you love yourself more. So, if it happens once, then the key word to use is No as in No More! Period. Then walk away and don't look back. The same applies to more mundane situations like your sister refuses to pay her bills before she goes out to party. Well that is her money and also her bills. They are not yours. You have set up a boundary that you clearly need to articulate to your sister when you are ready to fully enforce it. Then you have to mean it and not bend or break. You are not doing this to hurt her.

You are doing it to relieve the pressure off of you and to give her back ownership of her own problems and life. He or she has to be responsible for him or herself. Bottomline.

13. **<u>Prepare Yourself For Natural Consequences</u>-**
What happens when you pull a delicious bottle away from a hungry baby? They scream and fuss, right. Well prepare for your "Co-dependents" to act the same way despite their age! Yes, grandmothers, mothers, siblings, husbands, kids, family members and even colleagues at work might throw a serious temper tantrum when you are no longer willing to blindly give them what they want! I call it the **adult temper tantrum.**

They may yell at you, try to fight you, ignore you, refuse to talk to you (stonewalling), cry, curse you out, act out by hurting themselves- all the things that most infants do and more! You have to be prepared for the drama and the theatrics. This will go on for awhile because it will take awhile for them to realize that you are not playing with them and that you mean what you say. When they realize that you will not change your mind despite their antics, because you are letting them be responsible for themselves, then one or two things will happen. Either they will find someone else to "use" or be codependent upon or they will decide to be responsible for themselves. Many people that opt to stop being angry with you and look at themselves will often come back later and thank you for letting them fall so that they could get up on their own. I call it **Fighting The Mirror.** People will often prefer to fight the actual mirror than to look at their own image in the mirror. Either way, when you provide space for them to finally make some decisions on their own, it tends to be a wake-up call. **Here's the secret: You saving the day is not working!** If it is then, why are you reading this book? You're reading this book because you know that the way that things are now is not working and it is taking a toll on you but you don't know how to stop it. Now you know! You have to let go and let them be responsible for themselves. Either they will continue the fall which is their decision and their destiny or they will decide to stop fighting you and truly look at the mess they have created in their life. They will see how ungrateful they have been and how much you have done for them..or not. Either way, you then have permission to live your own life. **Let me say that again, despite whatever decision they decide to make about their life, you have now given yourself permission to live your OWN life.** The freedom that comes from that is indescribable!

14. **Seek Help-** Breaking the grip of Codependency is certainly not easy especially if you have been in Codependent situations all your life. You will most likely struggle with letting go and allowing people to live out their own destiny without your help.

This is even with the realization that the cycle will continue forever because if you don't stop then they will continue to not have to worry or problem-solve since you will keep doing it for them. So, why not have a blast while you stay up at night worrying. With that said, it is hard to disengage and to get off the merry-go-round. However, you can do it. If you find yourself struggling or backing down from your boundaries, which will create an even bigger problem once they see your weakness, then you may need to consider mental health therapy. Therapy is helpful so that you can process the origins of the Codependency and come up with a plan of action. Along with the plan of action, having some accountability to your therapist, can be helpful in helping you maintain firm boundaries. Now, the therapist is there for you either way and with no judgment but sometimes people feel stronger knowing that someone is in their corner.

RESOURCES

In the final section of **The Blindspot Blueprint**, I am going to list some tips and techniques you can consider using to help you through these emotional times.

And remember…I'm rooting for you!

<u>Possible Symptoms of Burn-Out</u>:

1. You are constantly tired.

2. You are mentally, physically, emotionally, and even spiritually drained.

3. You are angry and resentful.

4. You feel guilty about how angry and resentful you feel.

5. You may lash out at others inappropriately.

6. You struggle to concentrate and focus.

7. You are weepy even though you may hate crying.

8. You feel alone and like no one cares or understand you.

9. You feel like you are dying inside, in plain view, but no one sees you.

10. You are starting to fall back from your own responsibilities and you don't care what anyone thinks about it.

11. You want change but you don't know how to go about making those changes.

Self-Care To Prevent Burn-Out:

1. **Me Time**: Spend time alone or the way you want to for just you. It does not matter if someone understands why you need to do this or not. Just do it for your own mental and emotional health.

2. **Let People Be Responsible For Themselves**: Re-read the Codependency section if you are still struggling with this or get help from a professional as you start this journey. Utilize the Big B word! It won't be easy but it will be worth it.

3. **Figure Out Your Benefit With Everyone In Your Life-** It is time for you to be selfish. In this case, selfish is not a bad word.

You have given and given. Now it is time so to look around and figure out who feeds your spirit, who lifts you up when you are down, and who is there at crunch time when you really need them. Once you are clear then you need to start eradicating. If you can't stomach letting people leave your life then at least modify their access to you. This goal applies to parents, siblings, family, friends, partners, and colleagues. **Anyone that is not helping you is hurting you**. <u>Please read that again.</u> Now use it as a guideline as to who is helping you in your life and who isn't. You know what to do with the ones that are not helping you.

4. **Read books about Narcissistic Mothers/Parents, Perfectionism, and Codependency**. You don't have to take it from me. Knowledge is power! You can also watch some of my YouTube videos on these topics on my channel, **Therapist in Your Head.** The link to this channel is:

   http://bit.ly/therapistinyourheadchannel.

5. **Take Courses**: You will have to look for them but many therapists offer courses about the issues I listed above and much more. I have a couple in the works as we speak. If you are interested in keeping up with my course offerings, please consider subscribing to my email list,

   www.theblindspotbiz.com.

I will post the class on my website and link it to my Teachable account as they become available. I'd love to see you there!

6. **Affirmations**- In order to erase some of the negative dialogue that may go on in your conscious and subconscious mind, affirmations may be of great help. Affirmations only require that you say them to yourself to remind yourself of who you are aspiring to be day to day. Some affirmations that I use and love are below:

   a. I love you, <u>insert your name!</u>

   b. You've got this!

   c. All bets are on me and I won't lose!

   d. I will never be broke another day in my life!

   e. Spirit, please release anything that is not of you from my life.

I could go on and on but you get the picture. I keep them on my phone in the notes app and I make a habit of looking at them daily. I say them aloud or silently to myself. This helps to reprogram any negative thoughts that may lying dormant in my subconscious. Try it for 30 days and let me know what you think at **support@theblindspotbiz.com**.

7. **Mediation**- Practice meditation. This is a way to still your mind to hear your own thoughts. It is normal to have thoughts cross your mind but the more you do it the faster they move on until you are able to quiet your mind and get still. There are many ways to meditate. I often recommend to my clients with busy minds that they start with guided meditations.

The person guiding the mediation will help you relax by guiding you through a sequence of scenes. My favorite guided meditation expert is Kelly Howell. She has subliminal mediations and guided ones that are absolutely awesome. Check her out at: **https://www.brainsync.com/about-us/about-kelly-howell.html**. I have also created a quick mediation on my YouTube channel called the Anti-Anxiety Breath Exercise. Check it out today at: **http://bit.ly/therapistinyourheadchannel**.

8. **Yoga**- Yoga falls into alignment with meditation because it also works to still your mind by being mindful while you move and contort your body. Yoga has also been known to be immensely helpful for people who have experienced trauma.

Don't be surprised if you start crying during your yoga session!

CONCLUSION

A Word From The Author

It has been an absolute honor and privilege for me to write this book. I know firsthand how it feels to pull yourself from the depths of Perfectionistic tendencies and Codependent relationships, so to share my professional knowledge and well-earned knowledge is so fulfilling!

It is my hope and prayer that after reading this book you will begin the upward climb to your own personal freedom. That you will become aware of the truth of your situation and allow the truth to change you for the better.

This journey will take time. There is no quick fix but it can be done. You can live the life that you always wanted to live as soon as you make up your mind to start the process. Change is not easy but in most instances it is worth it.

The bottom line is that you must become resolute. You must make up your mind that this craziness stops TODAY. Awaken every morning with the determination to give changing your life for the better one more try, and then one more try, and then one more try until you look around and nothing in your life looks the same. Then my friend, you will be free!

Always remember, I'm rooting for you!

"Courage is not a state of fearlessness. Instead, it is about experiencing the fear and doing it anyway."
Unknown

Other Books By Deirdre F. Haynes

Nonfiction Books about Relationships
The Quick and Dirty Guide to Infidelity
The Cheatsheet: Who Are You REALLY dating?

Nonfiction Books about Business/Writing
The Quick and Dirty Guide to Starting Your Business
The Quick and Dirty Guide to the Effective Writer's
Mindset
Blindspots: Everything You Didn't Know You Needed To
Know About Starting Your Private Practice

Workbooks and Journals
The Big Book of Communications
The Vault: General Edition
The Vault: Therapist's Edition
The Vault: Group Therapy Edition
The Vault: Anxiety Edition
The Vault: Depression Edition
The Vault: Journal For Women
The Vault: Journal For Women
The Vault: Gratitude Edition
The Effective Therapist's Brain Dump
The Effective Therapist's Weekly To-Do List
The Effective Therapist's Daily To-Do-List

STAY IN CONTACT!

Deirdre F. Haynes, Ed.S, LPCS is a psychotherapist in Columbia, SC. She owns **Deirdre Haynes Counseling Services** and an online self-help and self-development hub, **The Blindspot Biz**.

To purchase any of her books, e-books and audible books on Amazon, please visit:
http://bit.ly/deirdrehaynesbooks

To Subscribe to her YouTube channel:
http://bit.ly/therapistinyourheadchannel

Deirdre Haynes Counseling Services:
Appointments (SC only): www.dhaynestherapy.com

www.facebook.com/dhaynestherapy
www.instagram.com/dhaynestherapy
www.twitter.com/dhaynestherapy

The Blindspot Biz: Online Self-Help Hub
(Products/Courses/Blog/Email List)

www.theblindspotbiz.com
www.facebook.com/theblindspotbiz
www.instagram.com/theblindspotbiz

Deirdre Haynes
P. O. Box 290902
Columbia, SC 29229

Printed in Great Britain
by Amazon